# Pandemic Era Poems

By

*David Glenister*

# TABLE OF CONTENTS

# DEDICATION

---

This book is dedicated to all who have suffered or lost loved ones during this COVID Era Pandemic.

# ACKNOWLEDGEMENTS

A big thank you goes to all my family, friends and the Sassy Book team for the help and input provided in the publication of this book.

# ABOUT THE AUTHOR

Since the Covid-19 pandemic struck in early 2020, the author, along with the rest of the country, has had to learn to adapt to updated regulations that manifestly changed how we socialised and worked. The changes affected people's lives in so many ways. These poems are borne during this turbulent period, not only out of the feelings, anxiety, and trepidations forced upon us by Covid but also by the changing nature of the environment, travel, and the weather taken as a whole.

My pandemic journey made me recognise that nothing can be taken for granted and that now I am more appreciative of the world in which we all live. I hope you can resonate with my thoughts and take some comfort from them.

David Glenister

# FOREWORD

The COVID-19 pandemic affected us in different ways, our accepted way of free-living vanishing to be replaced by unprecedented hospitalisations and deaths. With society under sustained attack, the very fabric of societal norms for gatherings such as celebrating a new life, marriage or death disappeared overnight. Everything pre-COVID we accepted as a given was replaced by regulations and laws. Living life in a goldfish bowl and working from home became for many the new norm. The experiences gained either personally, through media updates or by simply talking to friends and family left me with a myriad of thoughts, and so many unanswered questions. Slowly, as society reopens people are beginning to again enjoy walking in the fresh air and  perhaps other activities long forgotten. This book contains some of those thoughts explained in poems.

I have found it very cathartic writing the poems within this book, which you are perfectly entitled to disagree with.

Any views or opinions expressed are entirely my own which I freely share with you. Even now, though no longer regulated, we all still sit squarely in the eye of the COVID- 19 storm with daily hospitalisations and deaths albeit on a lower scale. The jury is out on whether we will ever return to life as it was pre-COVID.


**David Glenister**
1 . 11 . 21

# 01
# RULE CONFUSION

When Covid broke out, it all went manic
The government drowned in chaos and panic
With the country divided by the Brexit war
Λ control was needed - a brand new law

Coronavirus restrictions, whilst they were lots
Nobody thought of joining the dots
Conflicting opinions, from those in the know
Resulted in changes, that continued to grow

Forced lock downs and furloughs –caused some strife
Λffecting everything – our complete way of life
From birth to death and everything in between
Restrictions in place, felt ridiculously unseen

Government believes, we are all myopic
Rules changed, involving every topic
Mandated to wear masks, keeping social distance, and all
Yet for some not so much, eventually, it was their call

Contradictions and interpretation - making hardly any sense
It's either safe or its not – are we really that dense
Obviously not, the people voiced
Don't tell us what to do it's up to us – it's our choice

Too late for loved ones that now have departed
Family's divided and forever parted
Rules, lasted for over a year
A crucial time for sure; caused many a tear

Now out of lockdown, a brand-new dawn
Back to Parliament where MPs yawn
Our MPs return, for them no masks
Immune from Covid they go about their tasks

Masks made compulsory for parliamentary staff
Conflicting rules just make me laugh
It makes no sense to you and me.
Feeling confused? You should be.

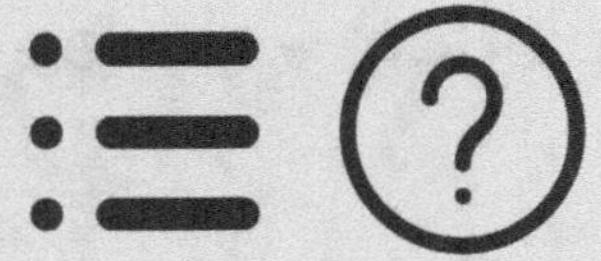

# 02
# RIP VAN COVID

From nowhere it came
It just appeared
Upsetting our lives
For a fair few years

Named Covid
A respiratory condition
That spread and mutated
Through an airborne infection

To manage the horror
Controls were set
Yet people still complained
So, control operations were not met


Covid continued
With deaths aplenty
People being weeded
A solution was needed

At last, a vaccine came along
It took two doses
Made people worry, caused alarm
But prevented them suffering from serious harm

An ongoing journey
A time tunnel of sorts
Like Rip Van Winkel
A few years older of course

Over time, we awake as from a dream
To a find a new dawn and hopefully some gleam
Going to work and forgetting the pain
We leave our homes again and again

Gone went the warnings
Masks and distancing
Controls all but vanished
Covid-19 not yet banished

With pandemic still present
For all to see
Management decided to
Invite us for tea

Don't' worry it's safe
We've won this race
Now get back to work
So, we can see your face

The fullness of time
Whilst that's still not clear
Will change the world
That we all hold dear

Was Covid a dream
Did it really happen
Is the world a better place?
Not really, It's the same rat race

# 03
# COVID ARRIVAL

It came as a blur
At the speed of light
A pandemic declared
They got that bit right

Named Covid-19
A virus they said
So small, and invisible,
Attacked all, leaving some dead

Where did it come from?
No one really knows
Worldwide now
What a huge, big blow

Nowhere's safe
All suffering; less or more
The people succumbing
Oh, what a chore

Despite best efforts, to kill it – not a breeze
Though everyone thought it'd be with ease
Λfter many months the virus still lives on
Sometime yet before it's gone

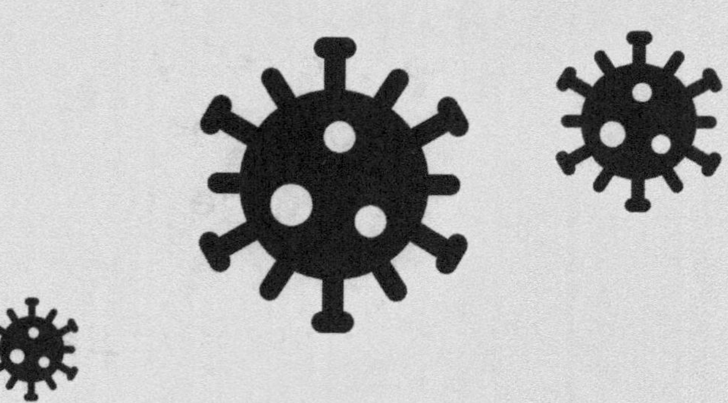

# 04
# WHAT PANDEMIC

A pandemic, are you mad,
That'll only make people sad,
Mankinds at war,
With what; not yet sure

A national lockdown – one big hit
We'll defeat the virus; bit by bit
With sabres drawn amid a lot of rattle
A quick win turned into a drawn-out battle

High casualty rates last seen in 1st World War
Covid attacked, the death rate soared
Back and forth in peak and trough
Caused people to worry; the going was rough

Month after month, the battle waged
The virus still there, in all its rage
Despite three lockdowns and all the pain
It's still with us and set to remain

# 05
# THE WEATHER

The sky opened up
Λnd water fell
In no small measure
More like something from hell

Λ single day, and a months' worth of rain
Grand indeed, it defeated the drains
Running down roads in one single file
Travelling a distance, maybe a mile

The rain then eddied; collecting in pools,
Entering buildings – built by our tools
The path caused damage and major destruction
That all now needs a costly re-construction

Λpart from the building, property, and all
People battered still. Yet, standing tall
Putting it all behind us is a bit of a strife
But bad things happen – now let's get on with life

# 06
# THE SWITCH

Brain spinning like a top
Can't seem to make it stop
It carries on, both night and day
Don't get much sleep; it goes without say

Updates daily, more infections and deaths
I keep saying sorry, just under my breath
A silent assassin causing viral plunder
All I can do is replay and wonder

News updates in a constant stream
My brain turns over as if in a dream
Thoughts not good, all so vivid
How do people accept and just live it!

For some, seems they accept the blues
Their brains wired differently; it siphons the news
A switch they have, they can turn on at will
For them, sleep doesn't need a pill

Alas! For me, that switch I lack
I need one fitted, to get my life back
The noise and news, for me, always bad
No sleep or break, makes me so sad

A life sentence until a switch is fitted
At least a prisoner may get acquitted
Can't wait for this bad dream to end
So, my life can start to mend

But for now. With my mind busy; not getting much sleep
I worry for the world and just weep, weep, weep

# 07
# THE MOUND

People stopped coming, to do their shop
Pavements silent, no more flip-flop
Oxford Street District, all but empty
Council income, hemorrhaging aplenty

Deafening the silence to make the streets sound
A plan was needed, and up came 'The Mound.'
A temporary structure – a great idea
Start the ball rolling – Let's get into gear

The cost acceptable, two million at best
Designed to attract people back to the nest
Design agreed, a large viewing point
Resting on scaffold poles hope not to disappoint

The Mound work started, so much to savour
Footfall increased, Oh what a favour
The build went on – longer than expected
Opening day long gone – not projected

Costs went up by a factor of four,
News got out, and boy did the press score
Poor management rife, project flawed
Λ councillor resigned, we were in awe

At last, the Mound finished
Its status diminished
No longer costing an entry fee
Λccess now totally free

The stairs outside to the platform led
Pigeons lying on their side as if in bed
Λrea surrounded with limited views,
Not breathtaking at all, or hardly news

Down I walk, oh what a mess,
Disappointment on my face Oh yes, yes, yes.
The Mound built to give the area a boost
Turned into a dovecote, a pigeon roost

Λ fabulous project, you may wonder.
Or a catastrophe. Λ great British blunder
Was it worth it - you may ask, why?
But that's a decision, for you and I.

# 08
# ENVIRONMENT BLUES

What's happening out there with the weather?
Seasons tan skin, like leather
All four seasons, now blended as one - the same
Is someone out there playing a game?

With energy demands high - a constant draw
Fossil fuels depleted – reserves now raw
Polluted air; global temperatures rising
Affecting seasons –not at all surprising

Government promises, gestures, a token
Sometimes completed, but mostly broken
Change is needed – now, not later
To stop the earth from becoming a crater

With oceans rising, at a rate
Island nations look to their fate
The rest of the world sits and talk
Time for them to walk the walk

Eco warriors bring environmental woe
To the Government – their identified foe
With the whole world now, in a rut
CO2, needs to be cut

They planned and then briefed their warrior force
Disruption of traffic – so obvious, of course
Attacking traffic during peak travel time
Some of them arrested for committing a crime

Sustainable energy; needed and fast
Fossil fuels waning; a thing of the past
Insulate homes, and use electric cars
Governments needed to raise the bar

Agreement reached; a new eco target
At least a commitment, something to market
With the whole world watching, is it enough?
Perhaps more demonstrations, that will be tough

# 09
# THE GREAT LIE

Simply put, it's where we are at
Each of us now, a Laboratory Rat
Unwilling participants, not our choice
The elected Government, our only voice

Our leaders, they worked it all out
The sums add up, it's safe to get about
No need for distancing; or masks
Go to work and get on with the tasks

So, what changed over the past year or so
Covid infections- still high, you know
Vaccinations, of course, mean less hospital admission
Eradication of Covid –it's the overall ambition

Covid resilient, so difficult to beat
A new approach needed to stop a repeat
Except people would catch it and possibly die
Build up herd immunity – that was the cry

Λ large-scale experiment was needed, of course
The whole of England was the source
Gone were controls to keep it in check
Go back to work –Oh, what the heck

And that's the great lie the Government sent out
Covid, still there and all about
For the experiment to succeed, controls must go
Otherwise, the results will be slow

We all are bit-part players, lab rats of sort
Being used by Government appears just for sport
With managers abiding by the Government lie
Workers forced to the office, and for some, they may die

Three months later and with the world watching on
Was the Government's information correct or a con?
Λ wave still forming –a tsunami maybe
Its the possibility of disaster, for you and me

Λnd the cost of this will come as no surprise
We pay with lives, watching numbers as they rise
The Governments fallback – the so-called Plan B
To return to controls sounds good to me


Λ brave decision, placing our eggs in one basket
Was it really to empty the grim reapers casket?
With results still unsure and not guaranteed
Let's hope the decision was not based on greed

# 10
# THE 3RD WORLD WAR

Few predicted a virus would be the foe
That its attack in force would create so much woe
With deaths and carnage to the right and left
The living left in shock and bereft

Λ global attack from coast to coast
Λ supply chain provided from an unwilling host
Don't worry; it's safe; few sad people scream
It'll soon fizzle out and run out of steam

With the ongoing battle in countries wide
Results ebbing and flowing–just like the tide
Death rates soared before they fell
Depicting scenes from Dante's Hell

At first, rules came to make us stay safe
Over time that started to rub and chafe
Businesses closed–they had no dosh
The fabric of life now under the cosh

Through mental anguish and personal loss
Λ mutated virus now showing whose boss
The war continued– nowhere to hide
Mankind collectively afloat with the tide

Like boxers sparring in the ring
Testing to see who's the king
No knockdown blow for either side
Just hang in there; for a bumpy ride

# 11
# HAM EGG AND CHIPS

Λ phone call from Gems it's really a plea
Can you please do something for me?
I've told my boss you're the best
I leave it to you to do the rest

Λ policy required – I need it fast
Must be up to date – not from the past
With the challenge accepted, and nose to the grind
I create a masterpiece; from blind

Sent by mail across the Thames
Where it was picked up by the Gems
That's brilliant, thank you. What is the fee?
Consider it a sample. I did it for free

Oh no, mister, payment must be made
Following discussion on what to be paid
Gems will pay when we meet on our trip
Breakfast on her – Ham. Eggs and Chips

# 12
# A FUN DAY OUT

The weather outside, windy with beautiful sun
Today's a day to have family fun
Into the car and off we ride
To a location, the whereabouts I hide

We arrive at Knole, the park of course
With diversions in place, that was a tour de force!
We spot the deer, so wild and free
Some of them try to hide behind a tree

Harems of doe, with young they huddle
Safety in numbers, as they cuddle
The graceful stags, now in their prime
Watch and wait for rutting time

Magnificent antlers so wide and tall
Bellowing challenges to others they call
But for now, they graze, play, have a lark
Secure within, their very own park

Prancing, dancing, free from strife
They seem to be at ease with their life
Today I feel free, like a deer
My mind is focused, now so clear

# 13
# BOAT FISHING

I've booked the 'Bonwey', an old fishing boat
Moored in Ramsgate, I'm told it'll float
Only Paul the skipper and just us two
Three men in a boat – so very few

With tackle and food enough for a week
We embark and cast off –glory we seek
Out of the harbour, and now at sea
Apart from the coast, not much to see

To the first mark, with lines baited
We start the fishing, for which we have waited
The first fish, a doggie, caught on squid
Not very big, yet it saved me a quid

From then on in, nip and tuck all the way
Catching dogfish and whiting, it goes without say
Then it's all change – a Sea Bass is caught
By my opponent, not me, for which I was wrought

To stick in the knife and compound my loss,
My opponent doubles up to prove he's the boss
At days end, we tackle down; head back to port
My opponent's the winner on this day of Sport

# 14
# ENERGY

Energy in all its forms
Now severely tested under the current norms
With firms under environmental attack
Sustainable energy not yet on track

Eco-warriors demand action, and now
Not quite sure exactly what and how
Insulate homes; I hear the cry
You'll use less energy – give it a try

Easier said than done
Those with homes were having none
No spare money to pay insulation
Now off on holiday, recuperation

Working from home, increased energy demand
Use fossil fuel energy; it's the Government's command
Oil, gas, and coal; the Grids burn
Out from the chimneys, CO2 churns

Deliverable, affordable; energy that's green
Λn aspiration, yet to be seen
Diesel and petrol, on the back page
Electric cars now all the rage

But people are fickle; they want what's best
Λs long as it's not them put to the test
Just look what happened when fuel pumps went dry
Drivers caused mayhem, enough; we cry

Governments blustering, agreeing to a man
Doing little, that seems like the plan
Our latest action, the ULEZ zone
Λ sup to stop the environmental moan

So, back to energy, demand at a high,
Costs going up, I hear people sigh
Reduce emissions, too high, not funny
Yet n the end, it comes down to money

# 15
# OBESITY BLUES

Covid strikes and lockdowns begin
It doesn't take long to get under your skin
Exercise limited, nothing to do
Except eat and play games, until your blue

It starts slowly at first; you don't see it come
Blissfully unaware of the size of your tum
And then the clothes- start getting tight
Putting them on is a bit of a fight

Food shopping online now takes hold,
Monthly bills trebling- if I may be so bold
Now we eat, every hour of the day
Getting fatter and fatter, it goes without say

Go on like this, and end up on a slab
Fitness regime decided, to fight the flab
Food intake limited to three meals a day
Along with some exercise that'll keep it at bay

No lockdown now, so getting out
I am so free; I want to shout
My weight gains now in full retreat
If only Covid were that simple to beat

# 16
# HOLIDAYS CANCELLED

Annual holidays, taken as read
When Covid arrived, they were killed stone-dead
Vacation plans all went to dust
Mothballed planes, now starting to rust

No sun, sand, sea, or the beach
No distant shores that we can reach
International travel, now all but banned
What other activities could be planned

With lockdown biting and everything shut
Nothing to do, but sit on your butt
We wait for the Virus to blow itself out
Weeks, months, and a year - it's still all about

A ray of hope to save the day
A vaccine created to keep it at bay
With proof of testing, being Covid free
Holidays' are now possible for you and me

# 17
# FUDGE AND LIQUORICE

I'm working from home; cats wander by,
An occasional meow but no mournful cry,
No wages earned, no expenses paid
Our furry friends have got it made

Fudge and Liquorice, but what's in a name,
Siblings both, yet not the same
We got them both as rescue kittens
Baby fur keeps them warm like mittens

Living with us, now for 12 years or more
They've earned a cat flap, their own front door
They sleep a lot; in cat years, they are old
I think they've begun to feel the cold

As pampered pets, they cost us money
Cathartic for sure, but oh so funny
And in return, who can deny
They make us laugh and sometimes cry

# 18
# LIVING ON THE FRONT LINE

It's hard to feel safe as a teacher in schools
Especially now, as there are no rules
The children mingle together and play
And do that constantly for most of the day

High absenteeism due to Covid rates rising
Teachers infected – that's hardly surprising
Staying safe - a daily chore
Wearing masks, Oh what a bore

Another teacher's sick, causing a flap
Call a substitute – fill the gap
With odds of catching Covid now high
It's no wonder that I worry and sigh

# 19
# FUNERALS

With the country under Covid attack
Regulations were brought in to start the fight back
Gatherings for funerals were limited or banned
Restrictions on numbers, that was the plan

Funerals planned – only eight to attend
No grieving period for family or friends
Don't chance your luck; just need to wait
The risk of catching Covid is great

The Virus robbed us of societal norms
Funerals for loved ones no longer conform
Alone, we now mourn those who have passed away
Thinking of them, shedding a tear as we pray

Time moves on, and regulations end
Families can now meet up and mend
But with Covid still there, it hasn't gone away
We need to remain vigilant and safe every day

Until fully safe and Covid free
No hugging or kissing; that works for me

# 20
# HOME LIVING

I worry, worry, worry and more
Look through the window when there's a knock on the door
Covid's the problem, and people as well
Taken together, they put me through hell

My home, a sanctuary, a Covid free zone,
Only family allowed, and that's set-in stone
With news updates daily and facts laid bare
What are the people doing out there?

The Government don't help, keeping it brief
Their take on Covid is causing me grief
Despite inoculations, I must ask
Why remove controls such as wearing a mask

When I go shopping, it's always a risk
I choose my time wisely, and I keep it brisk
Not the most enjoyable task
Always keeping my distance and wearing a mask

I leave the shop with what I've bought
Clean my hands lest Covid I've caught
Shopping into the car boot and out of sight
Driving off home, my face shows my plight

I'm through the front door, now safe at home
And yet my mind still wants to roam
Shopping placed into the quarantine store
I finally sit down and relax – until the next chore

# 21
# THE TREK

Like a Neanderthal hunter going out for game
I'm off for a walk, looking to do the same
No spear or weapons to take this trip
Just a mobile phone in case of a blip

I'll be wearing my utility coat –specially issued
Contains my masks, hand sanitiser, and tissues
I'm ready now, passed the final check
Its go, go, go, and I'm off on my trek

Front door opens; at last
I exit out and do it fast
My goal is to walk a mile or two
Where I'm going, haven't a clue

With the unseen enemy lurking about
I feel lucky just to get out
My head starts scanning, looking for a threat
Someone walking nearby; no problem just yet

I'm off, now out on patrol
Like an astronaut on a moon-walk stroll
My trek lasts no more than an hour
Nothing to report to make it sour

A successful day, I think that's fair
Walking about and getting some air
Now back home, everything in check
I sit and plan for my next trek

# 22
# THE NEW NORM

When Covid struck, literally in it flew
It changed our lives and all we knew
No gatherings, meetings or going out
The Virus was airborne; it was all about

Social distancing, masks and working from home
With National Lockdowns, no one to roam
The restrictions, though, came at a cost
A toll on businesses, many were lost

A new way of working, everything to plan
Anything iffy consigned to the pan
At last, came the vaccine, for all to see
Provided some protection, but we were still not free

Two years later, and not out of the wood
A change to the norm would do us all good
Means working together, all as a team
To defeat the Virus and realise our dream

Hybrid working, between office and home
Sensible idea, fewer people to roam
Keeping our distance, mask-wearing and all
Following guidance –still a good call

Electronic meetings, using Teams or Zoom
Communication assured, and straight to your room
As a synergy, less fossil fuel burnt
Protecting the environment as we have all learnt

For employers too, a chance to shine
Working with employees to keep Covid inline
With sensible controls and thinking outside the box
We can tame the Virus, get rid of this pox

It's a war for certain, a bit of a fight
Now down to people to do what's right
Enjoying life is still something to cherish
But don't let your guard down, as you might perish

# 23
# AUTUMN

Season's changing, the missing link
Λ living world, now in sync
I'm off to the park to roam and wander,
Λ seat I find so I sit and ponder

Time moves on, doesn't stop
With life going on, till we drop
I'm covered in leaves that fall around me like rain
Gliding through the air just like a plane

It's autumn now, the trees all on fire
Λ miracle of nature, something to admire
Λ bit of theatre, and all for free
Not a care in the world, I'm so full of glee

Though Covid is here – it's all about
It doesn't stop people from getting out
Enjoy the views, stay safe and follow the rules
Don't become a statistic like the reckless fools